D0350796

Totally Cool Caves and Hot Volcanoes

+10 more epic landforms!

by Janice Behrens

Content Consultant
Robbin Friedman, Children's Librarian
Chappaqua (N.Y.) Library

Reading Consultant
Jeanne M. Clidas, Ph.D
Reading Specialist

Children's Press®
An Imprint of Scholastic Inc.

Library of Congress Cataloging-in-Publication Data

Names: Behrens, Janice, 1972- author.
Title: Totally cool caves and hot volcanoes: plus 10 more epic landforms/ by Janice Behrens.
Description: New York, NY: Children's Press, an imprint of Scholastic Inc.,
2017. | Series: Rookie. Amazing America | Includes index.
Identifiers: LCCN 2016030322| ISBN 9780531228951 (library binding) | ISBN
9780531225899 (pbk.)
Subjects: LCSH: Landforms--Juvenile literature. | Geology--Juvenile
literature.
Classification: LCC GB404 .B44 2017 | DDC 551--dc23
LC record available at https://lccn.loc.gov/2016030322

Produced by Spooky Cheetah Press

Printed in China 62

1 2 3 4 5 6 7 8 9 10 R 26 25 24 23 22 21 20 19 18 17

Photographs ©: cover: Hyde John/Getty Images; back cover: Joe Carini/Getty Images; 3: Meinzahn/iStockphoto; 4: Science Photo Library/Getty Images; 5 top: Greg Winston/Getty Images; 5 bottom: Jake Rajs/Getty Images; 6-7 main: James L. Amos/Getty Images; 7 inset: Michele and Tom Grimm/Alamy Images; 8 inset: David S. Boyer and Arlan R. Wiker/National Geographic Creative; 8-9 main: Danita Delimont Stock/AWL Images; 9 inset: Matt Meadows/Getty Images; 10-11: Hyde John/Getty Images; 12-13: Michele Falzone/Getty Images; 14-15: Mark Brodkin Photography/Getty Images; 16-17 main: Left_Coast_Photographer/iStockphoto; 17 left inset: Alan Majchrowicz/Getty Images; 17 right inset: Stan Strange/EyeEm/Getty Images; 19 main: Russ Bishop/Alamy Images; 19 inset: Optical_Lens/iStockphoto; 20-21: manoa/Getty Images; 23 main: Ignacio Palacios/Getty Images; 23 inset: Momatiuk - Eastcott/Getty Images; 24-25: Inge Johnsson/Alamy Images; 26-27 background: ooyoo/iStockphoto; 26 top left: Mark Brodkin Photography/Getty Images; 26 top center: Stan Strange/EyeEm/Getty Images; 26 top right: Left_Coast_Photographer/iStockphoto; 26 center top left: Alan Majchrowicz/Getty Images; 26 center top: Danita Delimont Stock/AWL Images; 26 center top right: Science Photo Library/Getty Images; 26 center bottom left: James L. Amos/Getty Images; 26 center bottom: Hyde John/Getty Images; 26 center bottom right: Russ Bishop/Alamy Images; 26 bottom left: manoa/Getty Images; 26 bottom center: Ignacio Palacios/Getty Images; 26 bottom right: Inge Johnsson/Alamy Images; 28 main: JacobH/Getty Images; 28 sky: ooyoo/iStockphoto; 29 main: espiegle/iStockphoto; 29 inset: CJ_Romas/iStockphoto; 30 top: suesmith2/iStockphoto; 30 bottom: Peter Raven/Mark Custance/Alamy Images; 30 background: Eric Foltz/iStockphoto; 31: Danny Rivera; 32: Meinzahn/iStockphoto.

Maps by Jim McMahon.

Table of Contents

Introduction

Mount St. Helens, Washington

Boom! The top of the mountain blows! A cone with a hole is left in the earth. It is a kind of landform called a **volcano**.

Landforms are the shapes we see in the land. A mountain can have a pointy top. A plain is a wide area of flat land.

mountain

plain

There are lots of amazing landforms across the United States. Let's explore more!

Kilauea volcano, Hawaii
Totally Cool!
Lava can be 12 times as hot as boiling water.

Hot Lava and Cool Caves

Kilauea (KILL-uh-WAY-uh) is one of the most amazing volcanoes in the world. It has been erupting since 1983!

Each time, hot melted rock called lava spits out. It spreads out and covers the land. As the lava cools, it becomes hard rock.

cooled lava

Caves are another kind of landform. These wonders are under the ground.

Our country has the longest cave in the world, Mammoth Cave. It has secret rooms and hundreds of miles of tunnels. It even has rivers.

Mammoth Cave, Kentucky
cave salamander
Totally Cool!
Some animals that live in caves are blind. They use special hairs or antennae to feel their way in the dark.

Mendenhall Glacier caves, Alaska

Totally Cool!

You can only get to these icy caves by climbing over the glacier first!

Way up in Alaska, you can find the Mendenhall Glacier caves. They are inside a huge piece of ice called a glacier.

How are the caves formed? As ice melts, it drips into cracks in the glacier. The water slowly carves out the caves. They look like blue glass.

Rocks That Rock

Now, this is a big landform! It is the Grand Canyon. **Canyons** are made when wind or rivers wear away rock. The Colorado River began carving the Grand Canyon about six million years ago.

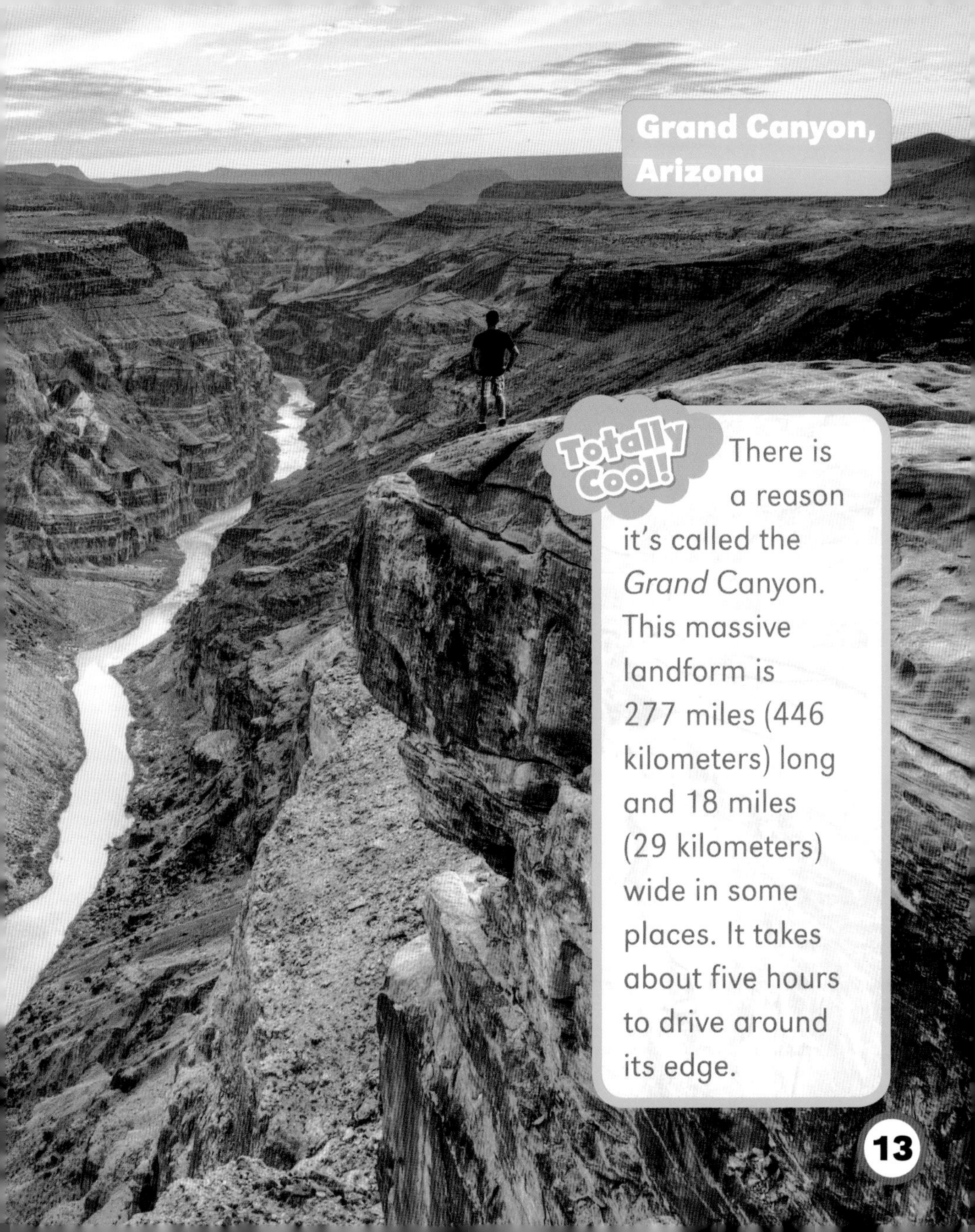

Grand Canyon, Arizona

Totally Cool! There is a reason it's called the *Grand* Canyon. This massive landform is 277 miles (446 kilometers) long and 18 miles (29 kilometers) wide in some places. It takes about five hours to drive around its edge.

Delicate Arch,
Utah

Rain and ice can also wear away rock. Strange shapes are left behind. A landform called an **arch** is one example.

In Utah, you can find more than 2,000 of these amazing arches.

Here are three more rockin' landforms in the United States. Try to figure out which is which.

- This is a canyon with steep, wavy walls.
- This is a **butte**. That is a high hill with a flat top.
- This one has a funny name. It is a **hoodoo**, which is a skinny tower of rock. Sometimes it has a rock on top that looks like a hat.

1. Antelope Canyon, Arizona. This is a canyon with wavy walls.
2. Makoshika State Park, Montana. This is a hoodoo.
3. Devils Tower, Wyoming. This is a butte.

1
2
3

Land Meets Water

The places where land meets water have names, too.

An ocean is a massive body of salt water. Its waves crash on the shore. Pounding waves create a flat piece of sandy land called a beach. There are many beautiful beaches in our country.

Big Sur, California
Totally Cool!
Waves grind rocks and shells into tiny pieces. That makes sand!

Niagara Falls, New York

Totally Cool!

The Niagara Falls belong to the United States and Canada.

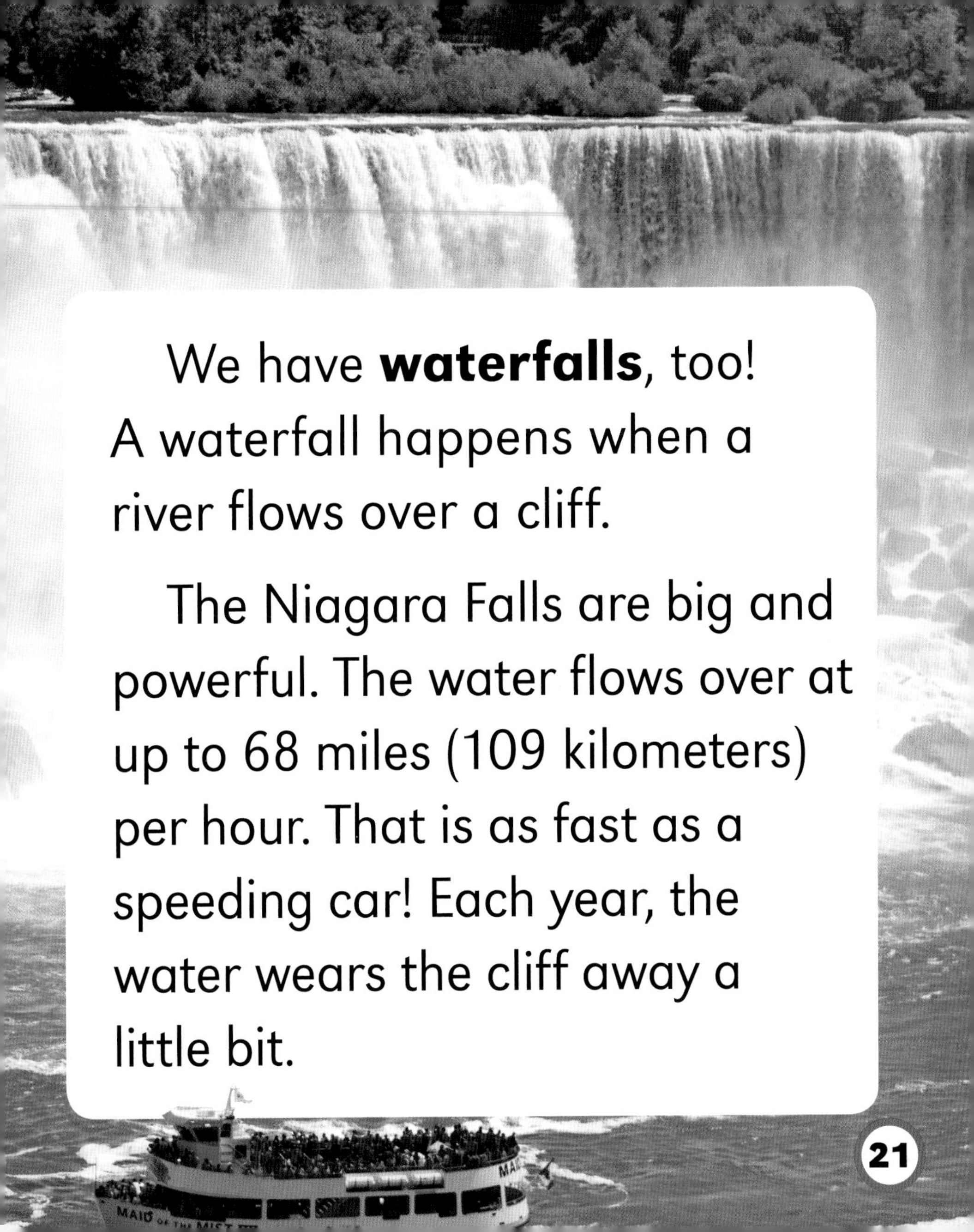

We have **waterfalls**, too! A waterfall happens when a river flows over a cliff.

The Niagara Falls are big and powerful. The water flows over at up to 68 miles (109 kilometers) per hour. That is as fast as a speeding car! Each year, the water wears the cliff away a little bit.

Crazy Colors

Look at the colors in the Grand Prismatic Spring! A **hot spring** like this is made when water seeps up from deep in the ground. When the water comes up, it is about 160° Fahrenheit (71° Celsius). That is way too hot for swimming!

The colors are made by tiny living things, called microbes, in the hot water. Amazing!

Grand Prismatic Spring, Wyoming

Totally Cool! If you visited this hot spring, you would have to stay on the boardwalk that goes along its side. It is too dangerous to walk close to the hot water.

Fly Geyser, Nevada

Not all landforms are made by nature. This **geyser** formed when people drilled into rock to make a well. Hot water from underground broke through. Fly Geyser's cones formed slowly. Over many years, minerals in the water built up into mounds.

Whether they are made by water, wind, or people, these landforms are something to see!

United States

Look at the number on each landform. Find it on the map.

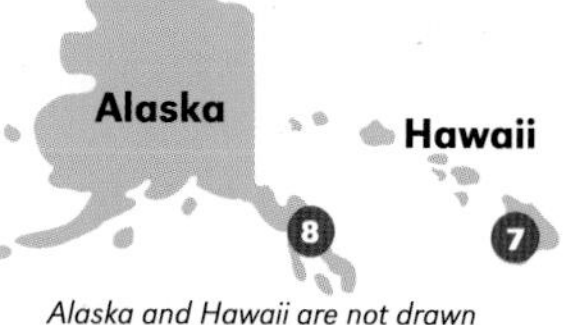

Alaska and Hawaii are not drawn to scale or placed in their proper places.

New Hampshire
Maine
Michigan
Vermont
North Dakota
Minnesota
4
Massachusetts
New York
10
Wisconsin
Rhode Island
2
South Dakota
Wyoming
Connecticut
Pennsylvania
New Jersey
Iowa
Nebraska
Ohio
Illinois
Delaware
Indiana
West Virginia
Maryland
Washington, D.C.
(U.S. capital)
Virginia
Colorado
Kansas
Kentucky
Missouri
5
North Carolina
Tennessee
Oklahoma
South Carolina
Arkansas
Compass Rose
Alabama
North
New Mexico
Georgia
West
East
Texas
South
Louisiana
Florida
Mississippi

Which Is More

Bryce Canyon National Park, Utah

- Bryce Canyon is filled with hoodoos—tall rock towers. The rock is an orange-red color.
- Mountain lions, black bears, and foxes live here. But they are hard to find!
- Local American Indians have a myth about the hoodoos. In their story, an angry god turned spirits called the "Legend People" into the tall stones.

Amazing? You Decide.

Turnip Rock, Lake Huron, Michigan

- This tiny island was made by waves. It took thousands of years to form.
- It got its name because it looks like a vegetable called a turnip.
- During most of the year, you can only get to Turnip Rock by boat. In winter, the water around it freezes solid. Some people walk on the ice to visit.

You Name It

Here are two amazing groups of rock that people gave funny nicknames. Can you guess what they are called?

Hint: *One is named after the biggest animal on land. The other is named after a famous cartoon dog.*

1. Parade of Elephants is in Arches National Park, Utah.
2. Snoopy Rock is in Arizona.

Visual Glossary

arch: a natural curved structure made of rock

butte: a rock with steep sides and a flat top

canyons: valleys with steep sides, carved by wind or water

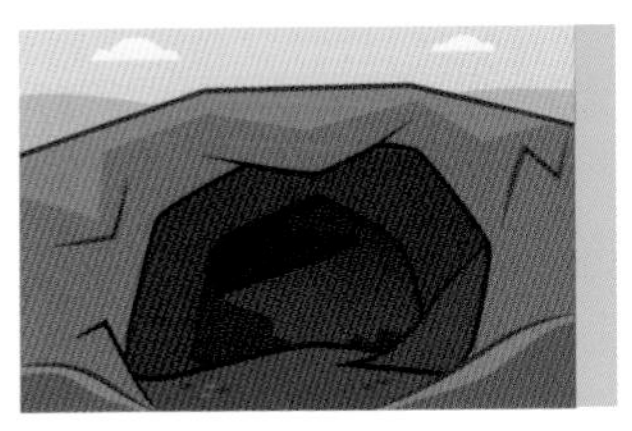

caves: enclosed spaces in the ground

geyser: a hole in the ground that shoots out hot water

hoodoo: an oddly shaped rock tower (often with cap rock)

hot spring: a place where hot water seeps up from the ground

volcano: a landform that erupts lava and gas

waterfalls: areas where a river falls over a cliff

Index

Facts for Now

Visit this Scholastic Web site for more information on caves and volcanoes:

www.factsfornow.scholastic.com

Enter the keywords Caves and Volcanoes

About the Author

Janice Behrens is an editor at Scholastic. She lives with her family and two guinea pigs in Brooklyn, New York. Brooklyn is on a landform called an island.